KING OF THE RAPPERS

by
Paul Davenport

Cornelsen

King of the Rappers
Paul Davenport

Verlagsredaktion
Sandhya Gupta

Technische Umsetzung
Peter Richter

Umschlagfoto
FontShop Berlin

Illustration
Oxford Designers & Illustrators

http://www.cornelsen.de

1. Auflage   Druck 4 3 2 1   Jahr 07 06 05 04

Alle Drucke dieser Auflage sind inhaltlich unverändert und können im Unterricht nebeneinander verwendet werden.

© 2004 Cornelsen Verlag, Berlin

Das Werk und seine Teile sind urheberrechtlich geschützt.
Jede Nutzung in anderen als den gesetzlich zugelassenen Fällen bedarf der vorherigen schriftlichen Einwilligung des Verlages. Hinweis zu § 52 a UrhG: Weder das Werk noch seine Teile dürfen ohne eine solche Einwilligung eingescannt und in ein Netzwerk eingestellt werden. Dies gilt auch für Intranets von Schulen und sonstigen Bildungseinrichtungen.

Druck: Saladruck, Berlin

ISBN 3-464-34397-9

Bestellnummer 343979

Gedruckt auf säurefreiem Papier, umweltschonend hergestellt aus chlorfrei gebleichten Faserstoffen.

CONTENTS

Chapter One 5

Chapter Two 7

Chapter Three 13

Chapter Four 20

Chapter Five 22

Chapter Six 26

Chapter Seven 29

Chapter Eight 35

Chapter Nine 38

Chapter Ten................... 43

Chapter Eleven................ 48

Activities 51

Vocabulary 53

CHAPTER ONE

Jason was a normal child.

Well, almost. There was that one thing: it was the way he talked. It wasn't just that he was a talker, one of those children who talk easily and talk a lot. No, it was something else, something his parents noticed about him at a very early age: Jason didn't just talk, he rhymed. He said things like "Mummy funny, dad mad" or "One, two, three, Tiffy in her tree." (Tiffy was their pet canary.)

Of course, with parents like his, Jason's way with words isn't surprising. William Stover, his dad, is professor of English at Northern State University. And his mother is the head librarian at the local library and spends much of her free time reading. They didn't say it at the time, but they both hoped that Jason might grow up to become a famous writer, perhaps even a poet. Later, when Jason was in kindergarten Mrs. Sykes, his teacher, noticed his way with words, too, and told his parents what a talented boy Jason was. The Stovers smiled. Yes, they were very proud of their son. And when Mrs. Sykes chose Jason to recite a Christmas poem at the Christmas celebration, Mr. and Mrs. Stover were even prouder. They were more nervous than Jason was about it, but Jason told them not to worry. He wouldn't make any mistakes.

And he didn't. When he finished, everyone was excited. They stood up and clapped a long time. Mrs. Sykes was smiling. Several parents went over to the Stovers and congratulated them on Jason's performance. One of the mothers said that she had often heard that poem recited, but there was something ... special about the way Jason did it. Yes, yes, said one of the fathers, it was the rhythm! Mrs. Stover told them that as a child Jason had started rhyming at the same age when other children started speaking.

What none of the parents had noticed was that Jason had changed the poem a little, not much, just a little, just to have some fun. He wasn't going to tell anyone about that, but when Mrs. Sykes looked at him through her thick glasses and shook her head, Jason knew that she knew. "Sorry," he said. "I was just having some fun."

"It's OK, Jason. I like what you did with the poem." She put her hand on his head and smiled. Jason smiled back.

From that day on – unfortunately for Jason – his parents began to talk to him about his 'gift for words' and tell him that he had the talent to become a famous writer some day. And regularly – almost every week – Mrs. Stover brought home a different children's book from the library with the same words: "Look what I brought you, Jason! You must read this!" Jason was too young at the time to really understand what all that meant, but as he grew older he began to realize what they were talking about and started feeling the pressure they were putting on him. Maybe that explains why he began to change so much – from an easy-going boy to a boy with more and more anger inside.

CHAPTER TWO

Life goes on and little boys slowly become big boys. Jason grew, too. And he was soon in junior high school. He wasn't what you'd call a good student. At least not as good as his parents wanted him to be, but good enough for Jason. He didn't like school all that much. The only class he really enjoyed was English, but he wished that his teachers wouldn't spend so much time talking about the ancient past, about stories and poems that were hundreds of years old. If only they would do something more modern, something that sounded like the way he and the other kids talked. Sometimes – not very often – there was a modern story, but then they'd go back to some stuff from the Stone Age and he would go on automatic pilot again.

It was a good thing school wasn't only teachers, classes and tests. That would be totally boring. It was a good thing there were clubs and sports and … girls, especially a girl named Dusty Rhodes, his best friend. He had known her ever since kindergarten when she and her parents moved into the house next to Jason's. Luckily she and her mom stayed there even after her father left the family. Oh, yes, school would be great if classes were only more interesting. But they weren't, so Jason – like most of his classmates – concentrated on the interesting part and accepted the rest. He thought of the teachers and classes as a fact of life, something you couldn't change. The most difficult thing for Jason was to stay calm when the teachers got angry and started shouting at him. He always wanted to shout back – and he sometimes did – but

Dusty was a big help to him with that problem. She showed him how to cool off. She was like her mom: always calm and relaxed.

But school changed for Jason the day his English teacher, Mr. Dibbins, announced that his class would take part in a national competition. The sponsor, the Department of Public Health, was looking for material they could use in a national anti-smoking advertising campaign. They were looking for things that would open young people's eyes and show them that smoking wasn't cool. A group of important people including pop and movie stars were the jury. There were great prizes. For the three winners there was a trip to Hollywood including a chance to perform their prize-winning entry on the Jay Leno Show. As usual, Jason was only half listening, but then Mr. Dibbins explained that the kind of material they were looking for could include songs, pictures, photos, stories, videos and poetry. When Jason heard the word 'poetry' he got all excited. POETRY! That meant rap to Jason and rap was playing with words, 'R n' R', rhythm and rhyme, and that was Jason's world. He decided at once that he would write a rap for the competition.

In the following weeks Mr. Dibbins' English class worked hard on their contributions to the competition. Some worked in groups, some alone, and a few, like Jason, worked with a partner. It hadn't taken him long to write his rap, but he continued working hard on it, trying to get it as perfect as he could. Dusty was a big help. She was his partner, his 'test person'. He tested his rhymes on her. Whenever he finished a few lines, they got together. Jason rapped and Dusty listened, and afterwards she told him what she thought. Sometimes she liked what he had written, but sometimes she didn't, and Jason had to make a change. But he didn't mind that. It was always

fun when he was with Dusty and working on a rap together with her was double fun.

The day before the students had to present what they had done for the competition, Mr. Dibbins asked Jason to see him during the lunch hour. Jason had just sat down with Dusty in the school cafeteria when he jumped up again. "Oh, oh, I just remembered something! Mr. Dibbins wants to talk with me. Wait for me, I'll be right back." Dusty waited, but when Jason still hadn't returned 20 minutes later, she left the cafeteria alone.

Mr. Dibbins and Jason were still talking. Mr. Dibbins had a 'problem' with Jason's rap. "Please don't misunderstand me, Jason, your ideas are good and you certainly have a way with words, but why have you used the rap form?" Mr. Dibbins smiled in a fatherly way.

"What do you mean? What's wrong with rap?"

"I know that this will sound hard, Jason, and I certainly don't mean all rap music when I say it, but so much of it is full of bad English." Mr. Dibbins' smile was still there, but not as bright now.

Jason laughed. "You mean the grammar? But that's the way the kids talk."

"I mean more than just grammar. What I mean is that a lot of rap music is like hot air: it sounds very important, but in reality it's empty. It's full of angry and dirty language. And don't say that's the way young people talk. I know that, but I also know when language like that is used just for show." Mr. Dibbins had stopped smiling.

"There is a lot of strong language, I know, but it's only natural to use language like that when you're angry about something."

"Angry? Of course, the rappers seem to be angry most of the time. They're angry about how bad life is in the ghettos, they're angry at the police, at politicians, at society, they're angry about everything! But the funny thing is, many of the same angry young men who are always rapping about their poor 'brothers and sisters' in the ghettos are the ones who drive the most expensive cars and live in the best parts of town!" Mr. Dibbins was talking faster and faster and moving his hands like … a rapper!

"OK, Mr. Dibbins, what you're saying is true of a lot of commercial rap. There are a lot of phoney rappers out there. And yeah, they make big money talking about things they don't know anything about, but there are black sheep everywhere, not just in the rap business. I know some teachers who are black sheep, too."

"Ow! That hurt!" Mr. Dibbins had to laugh. But he quickly turned serious again. "Maybe you're right, Jason. Maybe I'm not being fair. Maybe rap music isn't as bad as I think it is. But may I give you a little tip? What you've written is very good, but you'd have a much better chance of winning, if you changed the form a little to make it look more like a poem."

"Hmmm …" (Jason always said 'hmmm' when he felt himself getting angry. It was a trick Dusty had taught him.) "Hmmm, Mr. Dibbins, thanks for the tip, but let me try to explain why I can't possibly change what I've written. As you know, the word 'rap' means saying something suddenly and quickly, but it's also means criticizing something strongly. When you feel angry about something and you want to change it, rap is a good way to express your feelings. Good rap music is different than pop music. It's not about sunshine and love! It's a way of protesting against social problems." Jason stopped suddenly, surprised at himself, surprised that he was talking to his English teacher that way.

Mr. Dibbins was surprised, too. "I can see that you feel very strongly about this, Jason," he said slowly.

"Yes, and that's the way it is with the rap I wrote for the competition, too. It's about the anger I feel about the lies they put in cigarette advertising. It's my way of getting back at them. I couldn't write it any other way."

Mr. Dibbins didn't say anything for a moment. Finally he stood up, went over to Jason and put his arm on the boy's back. "OK, Jason, I still think you're making a mistake, but I can see that you're not going to change your mind, so go ahead with your rap and good luck to you."

CHAPTER THREE

The day came when the pupils of the class had to present their contributions. There was some good work. Sue Porter had painted a shocking picture of a smoker's lung, Leroy and Trevis Russell had written a song about a girl who beat the smoking habit, which they sang beautifully and Connie Sims had written a very interesting short story about a boy who had to choose between his girlfriend and smoking. When she finished reading it everyone went "Ooh!" and started clapping. Then it was Jason's turn. He was only a little nervous as he went to the front of the room. He had worked hard on his rap and knew that it was good. The others seemed to know that something good was coming, too. They were all quiet, even the ones who were always talking. Jason turned around and looked at the class. "Alright," he said. "What I've done for the competition is about cigarette advertising. You know, the kind with he-man models dressed in cowboy clothes riding across beautiful green prairies." Some of the students smiled knowingly. Suddenly, one of them whispered "The Big Texas Men" out loud and everyone laughed.

Jason waited a moment before going on. "They make everything look so clean and healthy. Of course they want you to believe that if you smoke that kind of cigarette, you'll be just like those cowboys in a world of freedom and adventure. Well, I've written a rap about the other side of those ads, the side they don't show. It's called 'The Missing Cowboys Rap' and I'm going to ask you to help me with it." When he said the word 'rap', the room started buzzing. Jason went around and gave each of them a copy. When he finished he returned to the front.

"Don't I get one, too?" It was Mr. Dibbins, who was standing in a corner.

Jason hurried over to him. "Sorry, Mr. Dibbins," he said.

Back at the desk, Jason waited a moment until all the pupils were looking at him. "Before we get started, I have to explain a few things. First of all, this rap is in the form of a dialogue. The parts of the text marked 'M' are for a man from the Department of Public Health, the parts marked 'T' for a group of tourists who've come to see the Big Texas Men. If it's alright with you, I'll do the Public Health man's part and you be the tourists, OK? We can do the refrain together. Would you take a look at the text, please?" All eyes in the room looked down. "As you can see, some of the words are written in small letters, others in large letters. The ones in small letters you say lightly and quickly and the ones in large letters slowly and loud. Let me show you what I mean. I'll do the first lines. Ready?"

"Ready!"

"'WHERE have all the COWBOYS GONE?' – Got it? Let's try it all together now, when I count to 3. Here we go: 1, 2, 3! 'WHERE have all the COWBOYS GONE?' – Hey, that was perfect. You got it on the first try. OK, so now I'll go through it once alone, just to give you a feel for the words and beat. After that, you do your part and I do mine, OK?"

Jason was a little nervous as he began and he even made a mistake (he said 'Big Texas Man' instead of 'Big Texas Men,' which no one seemed to notice), but as he went on he started feeling more and more relaxed. His voice grew stronger and his hands began to move. His classmates watched, fascinated, and began to move their hands, too. At first, Mr. Dibbins just stood in the corner and watched, but as the rap went on he started tapping his foot to the beat. When Jason finished, the class was about to clap, but he held up his hand and said,

"Wait. It's not over yet. This time you have to do your part. Are you ready?"

"Ready!"

> T: WHERE have all the
> COWBOYS GONE?
> The BIG TEXAS MEN, we mean,
> have you SEEN them?
> They were all HERE
> a YEAR or two ago,
> WHERE could they be?
> Did they just GO AWAY,
> go up in SMOKE and DISAPPEAR?
>
> Refrain
> T: BIG TEXAS MEN,
> Oh, BIG TEXAS MEN,
> handsome and STRONG,
> YEAH, handsome and STRONG,
> what went WRONG?
> with your HOLLYWOOD TAN,
> your PRETTY MAN TAN,
> WHERE have you GONE?
> tell us WHERE have you GONE?
>
> M: PUFF, PUFF, PUFF,
> they couldn't get ENOUGH
> of that BIG TEXAS STUFF,
> yeah, that BIG TEXAS STUFF!
>
> M: HEY, stay COOL,
> I KNOW where they are,
> I'll take you there,
> get in my CAR,

it's not FAR.
   We'll take a RIDE
   up the hill
   to the other SIDE
   down the hill,
   I'll be your GUIDE.
   Everybody out,
   just FOLLOW ME
   it's over THERE,
   behind those TREES.

T: Hey, WHERE ARE WE?
   Isn't this a
   CEMETERY?
   Is this a JOKE
   you're PLAYING,
   didn't you hear
   what we're SAYING?
   We'll say it AGAIN,
   loud and CLEAR,
   WHERE ARE
   the BIG TEXAS MEN,
   do you HEAR?

M: You've FOUND them,
   my FRIENDS.
   Big Texas Country is HERE,
   let me show you
   the BIG TEXAS MEN!
   Here lies SVEN,
   the LAST of THEM.
   On his right is MIKE,
   on his left JEFF.

In the SECOND ROW,
lie BARRY, LARRY, GARY,
JERRY and JOE.
Oh, yes, and BEN,
all GOOD MEN.
Big Texas is
PROUD of them,
yeah, PROUD of them!

T: It can't be TRUE,
we don't BELIEVE you,
they were so YOUNG
and HEALTHY, TOO.

M: They were YOUNG,
but had LUNG problems.
There's something WRONG
with the AIR
in Big Texas Country.
Not ONE reached FORTY.
The oldest was JAKE,
he was THIRTY EIGHT.
That HEALTHY LOOK
was the work
of their MAKE-UP GROUP.

T: We miss them SO,
the HORSES do, TOO.
They run around
sad and BLUE,
and look at us
as if to say
HEY! What went WRONG,

>   where have all
>   the COWBOYS GONE?
>
> Refrain
> T: BIG TEXAS MEN,
>   Oh, BIG TEXAS MEN,
>   handsome and STRONG,
>   YEAH, handsome and STRONG,
>   what went WRONG?
>   With your HOLLYWOOD TAN,
>   your PRETTY MAN TAN,
>   WHERE have you GONE?
>   tell us WHERE have you GONE?
>
> M: PUFF, PUFF, PUFF,
>   they couldn't get ENOUGH
>   of that BIG TEXAS STUFF,
>   that BIG TEXAS STUFF!

As soon as Jason finished the class stood up and started clapping and cheering and they continued long after he sat down. When they finally stopped, Jason turned and pointed at his girlfriend. "Don't forget Dusty," he said proudly. "She was a big help to me!" Immediately, the class started clapping again, just as loud as before. When the room was quiet again, Mr. Dibbins turned to the class with a happy smile on his face. "That was just wonderful! Yesterday I told Jason he should change his rap into a poem, but now I must admit that that was a big mistake. It's a good thing he didn't follow my advice. I think I've just become a rap fan!"

CHAPTER FOUR

Things happened quickly after that. Along with the other entries, the video of Jason's performance was sent to Washington. A month later the results of the competition were announced. Jason was one of the winners! A few days later a letter came for him. It was signed by a famous politician, who congratulated Jason and wished him a lot of fun on his trip to Hollywood. He also said that the Department of Public Health would like to sponsor a national tour with Jason. This is part of what he wrote: Would you like to make a tour of schools all across the United States? We will pay your expenses, of course. All you have to do is perform your anti-smoking rap. Excited, Jason showed the letter to his parents. Mrs. Stover looked at the letter but didn't say anything. Mr. Stover, who wasn't happy about Jason's activities as a rapper, only asked him if he was sure he wanted to accept the offer. Jason said he was.

Jason showed the letter to his friends at school. Several of them offered to go along as his 'manager'. They said he was very lucky to have a chance like that. "Who knows?" Dusty said. "This could be the beginning of a cool career. I can see your name in lights now: Jason Stover, King of the Rappers! No, no, that won't do! Wait a minute. What's your middle name?"

"James."

"Jason James Stover ... no, that's still not right. J. J. Stover ... that's it! J. J. Stover, King of the Rappers!"

The head of Jason's school, Mr. Rice, was a heavy smoker. But as the head of the school, he had to be a secret smoker. He did his best to hide it, but everyone knew. The students all called him 'Puff Rice'. He always had the window of his office wide open, even in the middle of the winter. Jason was nervous about showing him the letter from the Department of Public Health, but he knew that he had to. When Mr. Rice read it, he smiled. "It's OK, Jason. The Public Health people have already spoken to me about this. They said that if you want to go on the tour, I should give you my permission. Of course, as a non-smoker I said yes right away." Mr. Rice gave a nervous little laugh. "But you and I know, Jason, that you are not doing as well as you should be in school, and if you want to know my opinion, I think you should stay right here. What do you think?"

"Maybe you're right, Mr. Rice, but I'd still like to go on the tour. When I get back, I'll work harder in school. That's a promise." Jason gave him his best 'I-really-mean-it look'.

"You'll have to. Four weeks is a long time to be away. You'll have a lot of schoolwork to catch up on when you get back."

Mr. Rice gave a funny little laugh. He seemed to enjoy watching Jason squirm.

"I know."

"And you still want to go? What about your parents? What do they think of all this?"

"My parents are behind me." I wish they were, Jason thought to himself.

"Of course. Well, OK, Jason, with everyone for you, who am I to stand in your way? But I have a good memory. I won't forget what you said about working harder when you get back. Have you got a good memory, too?"

CHAPTER FIVE

It was shortly after Jason's tour was over when his father got the telephone call. "Hello, Bill, this is Lindsey," the caller said. Professor Stover recognized Dr. Lindsey White's voice and his heart gave a little jump. It was the first time she had ever called him. Dr. Lindsey White was the president of Northern State University and Professor Stover's 'boss'.

"Congratulations on your son. I read all about him in the newspaper. He's become a real celebrity!"

"Thank you."

"I read that he appeared at twenty schools in four weeks! Good Lord, Bill, that's a different school each day. He must be very tired after all that. How is he going to catch up on all the schoolwork he's missed? Aren't you a little worried about that?"

"A little, but – "

"Listen Bill, the main reason I'm calling is something else. As you know, this is Professor Fisby's last year. I've been talking with a lot of people, trying to find the right person to take old Fisby's place as head of the English Department. Uh, I know that you've only been with us a few years, Bill, and there are others who have been in the department much longer, but in my opinion what's important is how good a professor is, not how long he or she has been here. And you are good, Bill."

"Why, thank you, Dr. White."

"Call me Lindsey, Bill. Some people might say 'Bill Stover, who's Bill Stover, never heard of him'. But I have heard a lot about you, a lot of good things. What I'm trying to say, Bill, is would you like to become the new head of the English Department?"

"Oh, this is such a surprise! I don't know what to say. Yes, I would, oh yes, yes!"

"Wonderful! Uh, Bill?"

"Yes?"

"You might hear some people saying bad things about this. But don't worry about it. Universities are like that. There are a lot of ambitious people here, some of them almost too ambitious, people who think they should be the new head of the department and not you. My advice is just do your work and ignore them. Remember, I'm behind you all the way."

"I don't know what to say. I don't know how to thank you, Dr. White, er, I mean Lindsey."

"Well, maybe there is something you could do for me, and also for yourself. We were talking about Jason before. I'm sure that you want Jason to go to college when he finishes at Corona High School. I want that, too. In fact, I'm sure we could get him a very good scholarship. But, of course, he has to have good grades to qualify. And that could be a problem. He's not all that good in school, is he, Bill?"

"Er, no, not really, but he's still very young."

"Not that young. Jason's thirteen. Next year he'll start high school. Do you know what worries me, Bill?

"Not exactly."

"You know, Jason's tour was such a big success that I'm worried that he might be asked to do more tours. If he is allowed to do that, I'm afraid he won't be able to get the grades he needs for that scholarship. As I said before, being away from school for weeks at a time would make it almost impossible for him to keep up with his schoolwork." Professor Stover noticed a new, hard tone in Dr. White's voice.

"You may be right about that."

"Of course I'm right, Bill. And who knows what might happen to him out on the road alone like that. It's a dangerous world, believe me. You wouldn't want anything to happen to him out there, would you, Bill?"

"Of course not. I …"

"Listen, Bill. I'm a parent, too, and I know from my own experience what I'm talking about. Think about it. I know you'll come to see things my way. Think of Jason's future, think of the scholarship, think of your new position. And if the government people call and want Jason to go on tour again, you'll know what to say, won't you?

"I, er, I think so."

"Good! Oh, yes, about the new contract: take your time and when you've thought things through and you're ready, then call me and we'll get together in my office and you can sign it. Well, it's been nice talking to you, Bill. I'm pleased that we understand each other so well. Goodbye."

"Uh, Lindsey, I –"

CLICK!

For several minutes Bill Stover just stood there with the telephone still in his hand. The good feeling he had a few minutes before was gone.

CHAPTER SIX

There was a lot of loud talk and laughter in the air. It was the first day of the new school year and the students of Corona High School were excited. To first-year students like Jason and Dusty everything was new: the teachers, the rooms and the schedule. In the school cafeteria during lunch hour, they talked about their first morning. Dusty liked almost everything, especially her French teacher. She thought he looked like Tom Cruise "except for his nose."

"Whose nose?" Jason wanted to know.

"Mr. Lafayette's nose, of course. It's much longer than Tom Cruise's." They both laughed, but Dusty noticed that Jason's laugh was different than usual. When she looked closer, she saw that he looked a little sad.

"What is it, Jason? What's the matter?"

"You can see it?" Jason's eyes opened wide.

"I always notice when you're down."

"That's right. You do. But I'm not sure I want to talk about it."

"Come on, Jas. Maybe I can help."

"I don't think so, but OK, I'll tell you. It's about my anti-smoking rap. As you know, the Public Health people told me at the end of my tour that they'll probably want me to do another tour this year. They said I should be ready to go at short notice. Every day I've been waiting to hear from them. I've known for a long time that dad isn't happy about my rap tour, but he has always said that I'm old enough to know what I want and he won't stand in my way. But yesterday he said he had to have a 'serious talk' with me."

"Oh, oh, that sounds heavy," Dusty said.

"Yeah, it was heavy! All of a sudden, he starts talking about a scholarship! I couldn't believe it! He says I'm starting high school now and it's very important for me to get good grades. If I get As and Bs, I have a better chance of getting a scholarship, he says. I'm being cool, I'm going 'Yeah, Dad, sure, Dad,' and then comes the shocker! First the big question: If you go on tour, can you keep up with your schoolwork??? Then, before I can say anything, he answers for me: 'No, you can't! So if they ask you to go again, you've got to say sorry, but you can't afford to miss so much school.'"

"But, Jason, doesn't your dad realize what a lot of good you're doing? Doesn't he read the newspapers? What about all the faxes and e-mails you got after your tour? Doesn't he realize that you have the chance of becoming a famous rap star?"

"Ha! A rap star is the last thing my parents want me to become. What they want is for me to go to college so I can get a good job later on, something serious, not like being a rap star. But what they want most of all is for me to become a famous writer. They've been telling me that since I was a little boy!"

"OK, but you could go on tour and still get good enough grades to get you into college."

"I know, but they want my grades to be good enough to get a big, fat scholarship."

"Why is that so important? As a professor, your father is not exactly poor, and your mum makes good money, too. What's all this interest in a scholarship? I don't understand."

"I don't understand it, either. Not at all. When I was on the tour I called my parents almost every day. They wanted me to. Not because they were interested in what I was doing. No, it was because they were worried about me all alone on the road, so far from home. I knew they weren't really happy about the tour, but they gave me the feeling that they had at least accepted it. And now my dad says no more tours! I can't believe he's doing this to me. The tour was so cool. I met a lot of great people and everyone was so nice to me. More important than that, I had the feeling I was reaching a lot of kids with my message. And now this! It's all so strange." Just then the bell rang to end the lunch hour.

"I agree. There is something strange about this, Jason. I don't understand what's behind it, but I'm going to think about it." Dusty stood up quickly and picked up her tray.

"You are?" Jason smiled and felt a little better. When Dusty said that she would think about something, she did just that. And when she did, she most always came up with helpful ideas. Who said blondes are dumb? Dusty wasn't, that was for sure. Jason followed her as she put her tray away and headed for the cafeteria door.

CHAPTER SEVEN

With growing excitement, Dusty had read the article in the Corona Daily News about the plans to build a new gymnasium at Northern State University. Above the story was a large photo of the president of the university, Dr. Lindsey White, together with a famous architect, standing beside the old gym. Then she came to the part about where the university had suddenly got the millions of dollars for a new gym. Her eyes opened wider and wider. She read the words out loud: the money is a gift from 'Mr. X', a friend of the university who doesn't want to be named. Dusty almost jumped from her seat. "It all fits together!" she cried. She knew immediately what she had to do, the only question was how. Suddenly she thought of Linda White, Dr. White's daughter, who was also a student at Corona High. Linda's my best chance, she said to herself. Maybe I can somehow use her to help me carry out my plan. I'll have to keep my eyes and ears open!

The next day at school she got lucky. She found out that Dr. White would be away the coming weekend and that Linda was giving a party. She herself wasn't invited – Linda was a senior and didn't even know her – but it was a costume party, so there was a good chance of getting in without being recognized. Still, it was risky, so she'd have to be careful. It was important to choose the right costume. She suddenly thought of the clown costume her brother had worn to the Halloween Dance. It was perfect! It was also important to choose the right time to arrive at the party. The right time was when most of the others would be arriving. Not too early and not too late.

Should she tell Jason about her plan? She thought about it a moment and decided not to. He might be against it.

Dusty parked her bicycle behind some bushes near Dr. White's house and put on her costume. From there she watched the front door of the house for over half an hour until she finally saw her chance. Three or four cars had just driven up to the house and several boys and girls got out, all dressed in costumes. As they moved toward the front door Dusty hurried to catch up with them. When they were let in, she went in with them.

She knew exactly where the computer was. She had driven past the house several times on her bicycle the past few days and seen Dr. White through a window sitting at her computer. The room was on the first floor on the left side. But she wouldn't try to go there right away. She would look around carefully, size up the situation and wait for the right moment.

"Oh, hello." Someone was talking to her. Shocked, she turned around. It was another 'clown'. "I see I'm not the only one to come in a clown costume," a girl's voice said.

"Sorry about that." Dusty had prepared herself for this situation, but she still felt very nervous. "It's the only costume I had."

"Are you in Linda's class?"

"No, I'm not." Dusty was being careful. She didn't want to say too much.

"But you are a friend of Linda's, aren't you?"

"Not exactly. Can you keep a secret?" Dusty whispered.

"Oh, yes, I'm good at keeping secrets," the girl said. "Tell me."

"I'm a gatecrasher," Dusty said. Suddenly, the girl began to giggle nervously.

"What's so funny?" Dusty asked.

"I'm a gatecrasher, too," the girl said and giggled some more. "Why did you crash the party?" she asked when she had stopped laughing.

Dusty looked around as if to make sure no one was listening. "There's a boy here I want to meet," she said softly. The girl laughed again, louder this time. "What's so funny this time?" Dusty wanted to know.

"That's exactly why I came! I just hope we're not looking for the same boy. Is his name Michael?"

"No, no, it's not Michael."

"Thank goodness! Well, good luck to you – and don't get caught!" She gave Dusty a quick high five.

"Same to you – good luck!" Dusty stood and watched as the girl moved away into the crowd. She wanted to laugh out loud but she kept it inside.

Just then someone turned off the music. Dusty turned and saw a girl go to the middle of the crowded room. It was Linda White. She waited until everyone was quiet. "Now's the moment we've all been waiting for," she said in a loud voice. "It's time to find out who has the best costume. There will be prizes for different categories. First of all, for the best animal costume, the first prize goes to …"

Dusty couldn't believe her good luck. Linda was making it easy for her. While everyone was listening to her, Dusty moved slowly away from the crowd. She went toward the bathroom, but then she turned a corner and walked straight to Dr. White's office. She went over to the computer and turned it on. While waiting for it to warm up, she went to the door and put her ear against it. She could hear Linda White's loud voice.

When the computer was ready, Dusty clicked on the e-mails. Good, she said to herself, Dr. White does a lot of e-mailing. The list seemed endless. At first she saw nothing unusual but as she continued looking through the list, one of the mails suddenly caught her eye: AATD! Haven't I read something somewhere about an organization called AATD? She clicked it on. Right! It was the Association of American Tobacco Dealers! There was a short message:

Dear Lindsey,
Well done. The first payment for the gymnasium will be sent soon. Don't tell anyone where it came from. You can say it was from a rich man, a friend of the university, who doesn't want to be known. The rest of the money will follow when we're sure there will be no more tours. You have been very helpful!
Yours truly,
A. G.

Dusty was getting ready to print out the e-mail when she heard voices. Someone was coming! She thought of turning off the computer, but at that moment the door opened. She threw herself behind the desk and turned to look toward the door. She heard giggling. In the light from the computer she could see a boy and girl in each other's arms standing just inside the door kissing. Then they started moving towards her. The closer they came, the louder Dusty's heart pounded! They'll hear it any moment now, she thought.

"Hey, where's that light coming from?" the girl said.

"Huh? Oh, someone left a computer on," the boy answered.

More kissing and giggling.

Then: "I don't like this. Come on, let's look for a better place!" It was the boy's voice again. They were only a few steps from Dusty now. Her heart was booming like a drum.

"Do we have to?" said the girl after another kiss.

"We have to," the boy said.

"Are you sure?" They kissed again.

"I'm sure. Now come on! Let's get out of here before someone comes!" He pulled her by the arm and they left the room.

As soon as the door closed, Dusty waited a moment until she was calm again. Then she finished what she was doing quickly. When she had printed out a copy of the AATD e-mail, she turned off the computer. Then she went back to the party and when no one was looking she left quietly through the front door.

CHAPTER EIGHT

The next morning Jason's mobile phone rang and woke him up. He rubbed his eyes and looked at the display. There was a message from Dusty. Can you meet me in the town square at two o'clock? Important! He sent off an answer immediately: See you there. He wasn't sure what it was about, but Dusty was not the type of person who used the word 'important' without a good reason. Maybe she has found out something about why my dad won't let me go on any more tours. The more he had thought about his dad's strange behaviour, the less he understood it. Maybe Dusty has some answers to all my questions.

She smiled at him when he came along, a few minutes late. "Let's take a walk in the park," she said quickly. "There are too many people around here." They left the town square and walked toward the park. Dusty walked fast and didn't say anything. Jason noticed that she looked nervous. But when they came to the park she slowed down and began to talk.

"Let's go to where there are some benches. I've got something I want to show you," she said. Soon they reached the picnic area. They chose a bench where no one was near. "You must be wondering why I asked you to meet me," Dusty said.

"Is it about my father?"

"Yeah, it's about that problem with your father. I told you that I'd think about it. Well, I did. I asked myself why he changed his mind so suddenly. I thought about the reasons he gave you and I came to the conclusion that he wasn't telling you everything. I think he's hiding something. I decided to talk to my aunt about this – she's also an English professor at Northern State – and she told me that many people were surprised that such a young man was chosen for the job as head of the department instead of someone who's been there a lot longer."

"That's true, but dad said that Dr. White thought he was better than the others."

"I know. You told me that. But I still had the feeling that there was something strange about it. And then I read that the university had been given money – several million dollars – to build a new gym, and an alarm went off in my head! I now knew what I was looking for and where to look. I had to get into Dr. White's computer and have a look at her e-mails."

"What? Have you gone crazy? You could be arrested for that!"

"I know, but I had no choice. Besides, I didn't get caught. And I found what I was looking for!" Dusty pulled a piece of paper from her pocket. "Read this!"

Jason took a quick step back. "I ... I don't know. What you did is against the law, you know!"

"Sometimes you have to break the law. Come on, Jason, read it!" Dusty held the paper in front of his face.

Jason read the printout slowly. When he finished, his eyes were shining with anger. "The AATD is behind this. They gave Dr. White money to get my father to stop me going on tour again! And my dad went along with their plan! I don't believe it. Oh, man, that really sucks! I don't know who is the worst, the AATD, Dr. White or my father. Hmmmm!" Jason was trying hard to hold back his anger, but his face was growing redder and redder.

"Cool it, Jason. Anger is good, but control is better. What you've got to do is control your anger and turn it into action.

I can see two possibilities: either we go see Dr. White about what we know or we talk to your father." As usual, Dusty was calm and clear-headed.

Jason thought for a moment. "What do you say we should do?" he said finally.

"I think we should confront Dr. White with the situation. She's at the center of this whole thing."

"What about my father? What he did was just as wrong, wasn't it?"

"It wasn't the same. Dr. White used him," Dusty said.

"OK, so she's the one we've got to go after!" Jason jumped up from the bench as if he couldn't wait to get started.

CHAPTER NINE

Dr. White's secretary pointed toward the other side of the room. "Would you take a seat for a moment? I'll tell Dr. White you're here." Dusty and Jason took a seat in the corner. They said nothing at first, but after a while they began to talk quietly. Both of them looked nervous. After several long minutes the secretary's phone rang. She spoke softly into it and then turned to Jason and Dusty. "Alright, Dr. White will see you now."

When they went through the door to the president's office, Dr. White looked up from her desk and said hello. "Take a seat, please," she said in a friendly way. "I'm sorry that you had to wait so long, but now I've got lots of time for you. I understand that you're from the high school newspaper and you want to interview me about the university, is that right?" she said with her brightest smile.

"That's right," Jason said without returning her smile. Cool it! Dusty's words suddenly came into his head and he hung on to them against his growing anger.

"And you're Jason Stover, aren't you?"

"That's right," Jason said. Anger is good, control is better!

"Then your father is Professor Stover, right?"

"Right." Control your anger!

"Did he tell you about his new job?"

"Yes, he did," Jason said. Cool it, control your anger!

"Well, he's the right man for it, I can tell you that!" Dr. White smiled again.

38

"What we really want to talk about is your plan to build the new gym," Jason said.

"Oh, yes, of course, the new gymnasium." Dr. White was thrown off balance for just a moment, but then she gave a nervous little laugh. "Yes, yes, the old gym is much too small for a university as large as ours. Isn't it wonderful that we are getting a new one?"

"Yes, and how lucky you are that the mysterious Mr. X wants to give you the money to build it. Yeah, what a fine, generous person he must be. We'd like to know his real name for our readers, but he wants to remain unknown, doesn't he? That's what you said to the reporters, isn't it?." Jason gave Dr. White a funny little smile. Dusty was watching her closely.

"Yes, that's right. He doesn't want his name known, so if that's what you came for I'm sorry but I can't help you." Dr. White's voice had turned hard. "I – "

"Maybe we can help you remember the name," Dusty cut in. "What about A.G. or AATD?"

Dr. White got up suddenly, went around from behind the desk and stood in front of Dusty. She was trying to look calm, but her hands had begun to move nervously. "What are you talking about, young lady? Is this some kind of joke?"

"No. This is serious. Your Mr. X is none other than AATD, the Association of American Tobacco Dealers! And, of course, they have a very good reason for not wanting their name in the media. If it became known that it is the AATD who is giving the money for the new gym, people might start asking questions."

Dr. White's face didn't change, but when she spoke her voice was like a knife. "How dare you talk to me like that! If you don't say you're sorry right here and now, I'm going to have to ask you to leave my office!" Dr. White stared down at Dusty. Her eyes were small and cold.

Dusty returned her stare. "I have evidence," she said calmly. She handed Dr. White a piece of paper. As she read it her face turned red.

"I don't know exactly how you got this, young lady but one thing is sure: you did it illegally. And you and I both know that evidence that is obtained illegally is not acceptable in a court of law. In fact, it's worthless."

"That may be, but there is another court, the court of public opinion. Of course, Jason and I can keep a secret, but what do you think would happen if we told all our classmates what we know about your connection to AATD? Corona is a small town. How long do you think it would take before everyone knew about it?"

Dr. White turned away suddenly and went to the window, her back to Dusty and Jason, and stood there silently. Dusty looked over at Jason and noticed how angry he was getting. She shook her head and made a sign for him to be quiet. Jason understood and gave her a quick smile. When Dr. White finally turned around she was looking at Jason with sad eyes. Oh, oh, thought Jason, get out your violins, everyone. It's time for the 'Jason-I'm-sorry' part.

"Jason," she began slowly, "I'm sorry about what's happened, but I want you to understand what I did. As president of Northern State University I have to do what's best for the university. When I was told that we would be given money for a new gym I was very happy, but when I was told that I would only be given the money if I was able to stop you from going on any more anti-smoking tours, I didn't know what to do. I thought about it a long time. In the end, I decided that our new gymnasium was more important than your tour. Believe me, I didn't feel bad about this, but then I thought of a way to make it up to you. I got the AATD to agree to give you a full scholarship! Later, if you decide to go to the Northern State University, your parents won't have to pay a cent." She took a step closer to Jason and looked him full in the face. "I'm really sorry about your lost tour, Jason, but try to see the positive side of what I've done: your father got a better job, the university is getting a new gym and you'll be getting a full scholarship!" When she saw that the angry look on Jason's hadn't changed, Dr. White moved still closer to him. "I know you think that what I did was wrong," she said slowly. "Maybe you're right,

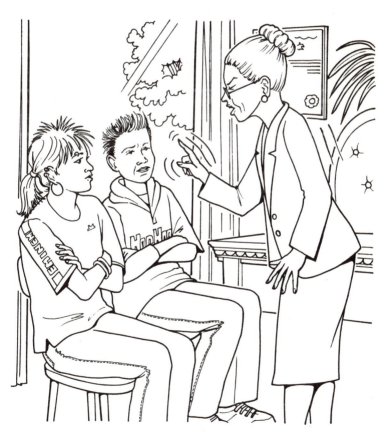

but what's been done is done and can't be changed. I hope you can accept that." She was standing very close to Jason now and looking him straight in the eye.

Jason just sat there. Dusty could almost feel his anger grow and was afraid he'd explode, but all he did was look around the room and say "hmmm." Good for you, Jason, Dusty thought. She could think of several things that she wanted to say, but she remained silent and waited. Dr. White looked at both of them and smiled. Then she went to the door and opened it. "I think the best idea is for both of you to go home and think about what I've said. When you've thought things through, just call me and we'll talk about it again, OK?"

"Oh, no, you've got it wrong, Dr. White," Jason said in a loud, clear voice. "You're the one who has to think things through, not us. And when you've finished, give us a call and we can talk about it again." Dr. White's smile disappeared. Her mouth fell open.

"But don't take too long. The government has asked Jason to go on tour again next month and we don't want to keep them waiting too long for the answer," Dusty warned. She was almost through the door when she turned. "And while you're thinking about things, don't forget what I said about the power of public opinion!"

"Wait a minute ..." Dr. White began, but Dusty turned and walked out, with Jason close behind. When they were outside, Jason stopped her. "What was that you said about a new tour?" He was smiling.

"Haven't you ever played cards? If you want to win, you have to bluff sometimes, don't you."

CHAPTER TEN

The days following the meeting with Dr. White went by slowly. Jason and Dusty went to school as usual and sat together in the lunch hour as usual, but they were nervous and didn't talk with each other much. They were waiting to hear from Dr. White.

A week after the meeting Jason got a call from a woman from the Department of Public Health. She asked if he would like to do a repeat of the tour. When Jason didn't answer right away, the woman asked if there was anything wrong. No, no, nothing, he said, he was just surprised. Of course he'd love to repeat the tour, but could he have time to talk with his parents about it? OK, the woman said, but they would have to have his answer within a week. Jason called Dusty immediately and told her the news. He hoped that she would say something that would make him feel better, but all she told him was that they had to continue waiting to see what Dr. White would do.

The following days seemed even longer than the days before. Jason became more and more nervous. He didn't eat well, he didn't sleep well and he couldn't concentrate in school. His teachers noticed it, too. One of them even spoke to him after class and asked him if anything was wrong. Then, the day before he would have to tell the Public Health woman whether he could go on the tour or not, he got a call from his father. "Can we talk when I get home from work," he wanted to know. "No problem," Jason said, "I'll be there." Has Dr. White said something to him? Jason asked himself. He could feel a bad headache coming on.

He wanted so much to talk to Dusty, but Dusty was home in bed with a cold. During his long classes, Jason tried to act as normally as possible and look as if he was interested in what the teachers were saying. After school, he had basketball practice. He played harder than usual. It felt good to run and jump and shake off some of his stress. When practice was over and it was finally time to go home, Jason's thoughts turned to the meeting with his father. He thought about it all the way home in the school bus.

When Jason arrived home his dad's car was in the garage. In the kitchen, his father was making himself something to eat. "Hi, Jason. Come on in. Is it alright with you if we have our little talk now?"

"Sure, Dad. What's it all about?" Jason started making himself a sandwich. He was trying to act cool.

His father went to the table with a sandwich and a cup of coffee and sat down. "I've got to tell you something. This is, uh, not going to be easy for me."

Oh, oh, Jason thought.

"I don't think you realize this, but when I told you there would be no more tours I felt really bad about it. I knew you would be very disappointed."

"Then why did you do it?"

"That's exactly what I want to talk to you about. I want to tell you the whole story."

Jason put his sandwich and a glass of milk on the table opposite his father and sat down …

"I'm listening," he said.

His father took a long drink of coffee and started telling about his talk with Dr. White. "After asking me to be the new head of the English Department," he said, "she suddenly started talking about you, about how important it was for you to work hard in school and get good grades, so you could get a scholarship to college. It wouldn't be good, she said, if you had to go on another tour and miss a lot of school again. And then, before I realized what was happening, she got me to agree to stop you from going on any more anti-smoking tours."

"So Dr. White was behind the whole thing!"

"No, Jason, Dr. White and me. I'm an adult. I can think for myself, but instead of standing up for you, I let myself be used." He took another long drink of coffee. There was pain in his eyes. "I'm surprised at myself – that I would do something like that."

Jason jumped up from his seat. Frustrated and angry, he hit the table hard with both hands. "I AM, TOO! DAMN IT, DAD, WHY DIDN'T YOU STAND UP FOR ME? YOU KNEW HOW MUCH THE TOUR MEANT TO ME! I CAN'T BELIEVE YOU WERE SUCH A WIMP! IT'S THE IDEA OF ME RAPPING. THAT'S IT, ISN'T IT? WHAT I WANT DOESN'T COUNT. IT'S WHAT YOU WANT THAT COUNTS. AND YOU'VE ALWAYS WANTED ONE THING: FOR ME TO BECOME A BIG, FAMOUS WRITER!"

Bill Stover sat completely still for a moment. He knew his son. He knew that he had to give Jason a chance to cool off. He studied his empty coffee cup a full minute before speaking again. "You're right to be angry. But you're wrong about the reason. I don't think that way. I am proud of your success as a rapper, really I am. But at the time, I really thought that a scholarship for you was more important than the tour. Now I know that I was only fooling myself."

"You fooled yourself and you fooled me, too. Yeah, Dad ... nobody's perfect, but don't expect me to forget what you did quickly. That will take some time."

"I understand. I would feel like that, too, if I were you. But listen, I had another long talk with Dr. White yesterday. She

was very unhappy. She's sorry about the whole thing. She said that at the time she was under a lot of pressure, but now she realizes that what she did to you wasn't fair. She wants to make it up to you. She says if I think you should go on tour, it's perfectly alright with her. You can't believe how glad I was to hear her say that!" He started to reach out his hand but when he saw the angry look on his son's face he pulled it back and smiled nervously. "I'm happy it's turned out this way," Jason's father said.

Without saying a word, Jason headed for the door.

"Where are you going so fast?" his father asked.

Jason turned quickly. "The Public Health people called last week and asked me to go on tour again. They gave me until tomorrow to decide."

His father smiled and started to say something, but Jason turned away and went out the door before he could get the words out.

CHAPTER ELEVEN

You ask, dear reader, what happened to Jason and the others after his new tour started. Well, as for Jason himself, he's not a 'famous rap star' (Dusty's words) yet, but he's off to a good start on a 'cool career' (again Dusty's words). Besides his two successful tours, he's been on the Jay Leno Show again and – he's really excited about this – MTV is interested in making a show with him. Yes, and that second tour was even bigger and better than the first. He was sent to larger schools and performed for larger audiences. Jason had learned a lot on his first tour, and on his second tour his audiences were even more enthusiastic than the first time. But, when he got back home it wasn't easy for him to forget the excitement of the tour and return to his life as a 'normal' student.

It was a big help to be able to discuss that problem with his father. During the tour, the two of them had come closer to each other again and by the time Jason returned home, their relationship was better than ever. His father had learned to accept the fact that Jason was a rapper, not a writer. And he took more time for him now than in the past. (Maybe he was trying harder because of the wrong he had done to Jason.) Anyway, they talked more often now and their talks were good for Jason: they helped him calm down and concentrate on his everyday life again.

And Dusty? Dusty is no longer Jason's girlfriend. It happened while Jason was on tour. Four weeks are a long time and Dusty is a very active girl. She met Darren at a dance. She still wants to be Jason's friend, she told him, and she even said that she would help him with new rap texts. But Jason has a new 'test person' now – her name is Sally, a really good-looking and intelligent girl with a nice figure – so he doesn't need Dusty's help any more.

And Jason's dad? He's become a very good head of the English Department. At least he's made a very good start. It wasn't easy for him the first few weeks on his new job. Some of the older professors who thought they should be the new head weren't very friendly to Professor Stover for a while. But he's always such a friendly guy himself, the kind of person it's hard to stay mad at even if you want to, that it wasn't long before he was accepted by almost everyone.

What about Dr. White, you ask. Well, Dr. White gave a press conference in which she said that the new gymnasium wouldn't be built after all. The whole thing about Mr. X had turned out to be a hoax. Someone had played a mean trick on her, clearly someone who had something against the university. Maybe it was someone who had been thrown out or who had failed their exams. Whoever he was, she said, he was a very clever person who had made her and everyone else believe that he was really going to give the university all that money for a new gymnasium. She was very sorry about the whole thing, Dr. White said, and she hoped that one day soon they would have enough money for the gym without Mr. X. She wanted to end the press conference right there, but then came the questions. Who was this Mr. X? How did she know that it was a man? Had she talked with him? How often? How old did she think he was? Did he have an accent? Had he said anything about why he wanted to give the money? Etc. etc. At first, Dr. White was calm and answered the questions smoothly. But the more questions the reporters threw at her, the more nervous she became. First her neck grew red, then her face. In the end, she threw up her hands. "NO MORE

QUESTIONS!" she shouted and left the room in a hurry. Of course, the photo of her press conference in the next day's Corona Daily was not of her looking good in the first part of the conference, but of her with her hands in the air and her mouth wide open at the end of the conference. What she was saying was printed under the photo in extra large letters: NO MORE QUESTIONS! The following weeks weren't easy for Dr. White.

I hope, dear reader, that I've answered all your questions. There's really not much more I can tell you right now. If you want to know more, you'll just have to wait until Jason gets a little older.

Oh, perhaps there is one more thing I could add. It's about Jason's newest rap. The Department of Public Health called him yesterday and asked him to write a new anti-smoking rap for his next tour. Jason got started on it right away and with Sally's help he has already finished the first verse. It goes like this:

> I'd walk a MILE
> for a DRAGON
> cross the NILE
> for a DRAGON,
> for a DRAG ON
> a DRAGON.
> for a DRAGON,
> to PUFF
> on a DRAGON –
> If I COULD
> if I only COULD
> but I WOULDN'T get far
> on my LEG of WOOD!

ACTIVITIES

Chapter 1
Can you write a short text about a child like Jason, who is 'normal' except for one thing? You can use any name you'd like, for example: *Corinne was a normal child except for ...* (her fingers? the way she slept?)

Chapter 2
Write or make something (poster, video, photo, rap, etc.) for the ANTI-SMOKING CAMPAIGN.

Chapter 3
Together with a partner memorize the verses and the refrain of the rap and perform it without using the text.

Chapter 4
Imagine that you and your partner have decided to become rappers. Try to find 3 attractive new 'rapper' names for yourselves. Explain why you have chosen them.

Chapter 5
Why does Dr. White want Jason to stop going on tour again?

Chapter 6
Imagine that you are Jason. Choose a partner to be Dusty, and explain to her why you are so disappointed. Try to say as much as you can without looking at your text. When you finish, you change the roles: your partner is Jason and you are Dusty.

Chapter 7
Act out the scene at the party with your class. First, you make

a list of all the roles. Second, you find out who wants to play which role. Third, take some time to practice your role, what you have to say and do. Finally, you're ready to play the scene. The teacher or a student can be the 'director', responsible for organizing the scenes, for example by deciding how the room should be changed, by showing the 'actors' where they must stand, how they must talk, etc.

Chapter 8
Write down what Dusty found out from the following sources: a) the newspaper; b) her aunt; c) Dr. White's e-mail

Chapter 9
Draw a picture of the secretary's and the president's offices next to each other including all the parts (door, window, etc.) mentioned in the text. Using a different colour for Jason, Dusty and Dr. White, make arrows showing their movements from the beginning to the end of the chapter.

Chapter 10
Imagine that you are Jason's mother. Jason comes to you after his talk with his father and tells you what a wimp his father is. Think about what you would tell Jason. Write down 3 or 4 sentences.

Chapter 11
Write a short personal comment on what is said about what has become of the people in the story. You could write something like this: *I think it's good that Jason and his father have become friends again ...*

VOCABULARY

Abbreviations: s.p. = simple past (einfache Vergangenheit)
p.p. = past participle (Partizip Perfekt)
sb. = somebody
sth. = something

A
about: What's it all about? Um was geht es?
accent ['æksent] Akzent
(to) **accept** [ək'sept] akzeptieren, annehmen
acceptable [ək'septəbl] zulässig; akzeptabel
(to) **admit** [əd'mɪt] zugeben
(to) **afford** [ə'fɔːd] leisten
after all: it wouldn't be built after all es würde nun doch nicht gebaut
afterwards ['ɑːftəwədz] danach
alarm [ə'lɑːm]: **an alarm went off in her head** die Alarmglocken läuteten bei ihr
all: he didn't like it all that much er mochte es nicht besonders; **all the way** den ganzen Weg; **not all that good** nicht ganz so gut
along mit; (to) **come along** auf jemanden zu kommen; mitkommen; (to) **go along** mitgehen
alright [ɔːl'raɪt] in Ordnung; **Is it alright with you?** Findest du es in Ordnung?
ambitious [æm'bɪʃəs] ehrgeizig
ancient: ancient past ['eɪnʃənt] längst vergangene Zeiten
anger ['æŋgə] Wut
(to) **announce** [ə'naʊns] ankündigen
architect ['ɑːkɪtekt] Architekt
As [eɪz] **and Bs** [biːz] (Schul-) Note 1 und 2
as for Jason himself was Jason betrifft
association [əsəʊsi'eɪʃn] Vereinigung, Verband
automatic pilot ['ɔːtə'mætɪk 'paɪlət] Autopilot

B
balance: (to) **be thrown off balance** aus dem Gleichgewicht gebracht werden
beat [biːt]: 1. Rhythmus; 2. s.p. (to) **beat the smoking habit** sich das Rauchen abgewöhnen
behind: they are behind me sie stehen hinter mir, sie unterstützen mich
bell [bel] Klingel
blondes [blɒndz] Blondinen
blue traurig
(to) **bluff** [blʌf] bluffen
(to) **boom** [buːm] trommeln
(to) **buzz** [bʌz]: **the room started buzzing** im Zimmer begann es lebendig zu werden
by: by the time als; (to) **go by** vorbeigehen

C
caller ['kɔːlə] Anrufer/in
calm [kɑːm] ruhig; **calm down** sich beruhigen
came: s.p. (to) **come up with** kommen auf, einfallen
canary [kə'neəri] Kanarienvogel
(to) **carry out** ausführen
(to) **catch up** nachholen; (to) **catch up with sb.** jem. einholen
caught: s.p. (to) **catch her eye** auf etwas aufmerksam werden
celebrity [sə'lebrəti] Berühmtheit
cemetery ['semətri] Friedhof

certainly ['sɜːtnli] sicherlich
(to) **change one's mind** seine Meinung ändern
clear-headed [klɪə'hedəd] klar denkend
clearly ['klɪəli] klar, eindeutig
Click [klɪk] Klick
closely ['kləʊsli] nahe
(to) **come: Come on in!** Komm doch herein! **A headache is coming on** Ich beginne Kopfschmerzen zu bekommen
commercial [kə'mɜːʃl] vermarktet
conclusion [kən'kluːʒn] Schlussfolgerung
(to) **confront** [kən'frʌnt] konfrontieren
(to) **congratulate (on)** [kən'grætʃuleɪt] gratulieren (zu)
(to) **continue** [kən'tɪnjuː] fortfahren, weitermachen
contribution [kɒntrɪ'bjuːʃn] Beitrag
Cool it [kuːl] Beruhige dich
court [kɔːt] Gericht; **court of public opinion** das Gericht der öffentlichen Meinung
(to) **crash a party** [kræʃ] uneingeladen zu einer Party gehen
crowded ['kraʊdɪd] voll (mit Menschen)
(to) **cut in** unterbrechen

D
damn it ['dæm ɪt] verdammt
(to) **dare** [deə] wagen, sich trauen
dealer ['diːlə] Händler
department [dɪ'pɑːtmənt] Fachbereich; **Department of Public Health** Gesundheitsbehörde; **English Department** Fachbereich Englisch (an einer Hochschule)
disappointed [dɪsə'pɔɪntɪd] enttäuscht
display [dɪ'spleɪ] optische (Daten-)Anzeige
double fun [dʌbl fʌn] doppelter Spaß
down niedergeschlagen; (to) **slow down** langsamer werden; (to) **calm down** sich beruhigen

(to) **drag on** [dræg] einen Zug (von einer Zigarette) nehmen
dragon ['drægən] Drachen
drink Schluck
dumb [dʌm] dumm, doof

E
easy-going gelassen, ruhig
endless endlos
enthusiastic [ɪnθjuːziː'æstɪk] begeistert
everyday life Alltagsleben
evidence ['evɪdəns] Beweis
except [ɪk'sept] außer
excitement [ɪk'saɪtmənt] Aufregung
expense [ɪk'spens] Ausgabe

F
fascinated ['fæsɪneɪtɪd] fasziniert
(to) **fool oneself** [fuːl] sich etwas vormachen
for: for sure sicher; **for weeks at a time** wochenlang
freedom ['friːdəm] Freiheit

G
gatecrasher ['geɪtkræʃə] ungeladener Gast
generous ['dʒenərəs] großzügig
(to) **get:** (to) **get caught** erwischt werden; (to) **get sth. wrong** etwas falsch verstehen; (to) **get lucky** Glück haben; (to) **get sb. to do sth.** jemanden dazu bringen etwas zu tun; (to) **get started** beginnen; (to) **get back at sb.** jemandem etwas heimzahlen
(to) **giggle** ['gɪgl] kichern
(to) **give sb. a call** jem. anrufen
(to) **go:** (to) **go after sb.** jem. verfolgen, sich jem. vorknöpfen; (to) **go ahead** weitermachen; (to) **go along** mitkommen; **I'm going "…"** Ich sage: „…"; **it goes like this** es geht so
good: good for you gut, prima; **a lot of good** viel Gutes
grew [gruː]: *s.p.* (to) **grow** werden
gymnasium [dʒɪm'neɪziəm] Turnhalle

H
(to) **hand sb. sth.** jem. etwas reichen, jem. etwas (über)geben
handsome ['hænsəm] gutaussehend
(to) **have a way with words** sich gut ausdrücken können
head: 1. Direktor/in; Leiter/in; **2.** (to) **head for** zugehen auf, gehen zu; **head librarian** [laɪˈbreəriən] Chefbibliothekarin
heavy ['hevi] **1.** stark; **2.** ernst
helpful ['helpfl] hilfsbereit
he-man ein richtiger Mann
Here we go Los geht's
(to) **hide** [haɪd] verstecken
high five *eine Art Siegeszeichen, bei dem zwei Personen sich mit hochgestrecktem Arm in die Hände schlagen*
hoax [həʊks] Streich, Trick
hung on [hʌŋ]: *s.p.* (to) **hang on** festhalten
hurry: in a hurry eilig, schnell

I
(to) **ignore** [ɪgˈnɔː] ignorieren
immediately [ɪˈmiːdiətlɪ] sofort, gleich

J
jury ['dʒʊəri] Jury, Preisgericht

K
(to) **keep:** (to) **keep sb. waiting** jem. warten lassen; (to) **keep up with** mithalten; den Anschluss behalten

L
lie [laɪ] Lüge
light: in lights in Leuchtschrift
look: (to) **take a look at** sich ansehen
Lord: Good Lord mein Gott, meine Güte
lung [lʌŋ] Lunge

M
(to) **make:** (to) **make it up to sb.** es bei jemandem wieder gutmachen; (to) **make sure** sicher gehen
matter: What's the matter? Was ist los?
mean [miːn] gemein
memory ['meməri] Gedächtnis
(to) **misunderstand** [mɪsʌndəˈstænd] missverstehen

N
Nile [naɪl] *(der Fluss)* Nil
none other kein anderer
notice: at short notice kurzfristig

O
off: he's off to er ist auf dem Weg zu
on the first try beim ersten Versuch

P
past: ancient past längst vergangene Zeiten
payment ['peɪmənt] Bezahlung
performance [pəˈfɔːməns] Vorführung
permission [pəˈmɪʃn] Erlaubnis
phoney ['fəʊni] unecht
poet ['pəʊɪt] Dichter
possibly: I can't possibly change this ich kann dies unmöglich ändern
(to) **pound** [paʊnd] klopfen
practice ['præktɪs] Training
prairie ['preəri] Prärie
pressure ['preʃə]: (to) **put pressure on sb.** jemanden unter Druck setzen; (to) **be under pressure** unter Druck sein
printout ['prɪntaʊt] Ausdruck
(to) **puff** [pʌf] paffen

Q
(to) **qualify** ['kwɒlɪfaɪ] qualifizieren

R
(to) **reach out** ausstrecken
reality [riˈæləti] Wirklichkeit
(to) **recite** [riˈsaɪt] vortragen
refrain [rɪˈfreɪn] Refrain
(to) **remain** [rɪˈmeɪn] bleiben
repeat [rɪˈpiːt] **1.** Wiederholung; **2.** (to) **repeat** wiederholen
right genau; **right away** sofort

risky [ˈrɪski] riskant
(to) **rub** [rʌb] reiben

S

seat [siːt] Sitz; (to) **take a seat** sich (hin-)setzen
(to) **shake off** [ʃeɪk] abschütteln
shocker [ˈʃɒkə] Schocker, schockierendes Erlebnis
short: at short notice [ˈnəʊtɪs] kurzfristig; **shortly after** kurz nach
show: it is used for show es wird benutzt, um Eindruck zu machen
(to) **size up** [saɪz] abschätzen
smoothly [ˈsmuːðli] ruhig
softly [ˈsɒftli] leise
square [skweə]: **town square** Platz (in einer Stadt)
(to) **squirm** [skɜːm] sich drehen und winden
(to) **stand up for sb.** für jem. eintreten
stare [steə] 1. (starrer) Blick; 2. (to) **stare** starren; (to) **stare down** nach unten starren
still [stɪl] still, regungslos
stood up [stʊd]: *s.p.* (to) **stand up** aufstehen
studied [ˈstʌdɪd]: *s.p.* (to) **study** genau ansehen, untersuchen
(to) **suck** [sʌk]: **that sucks** das nervt
sudden [ˈsʌdn]: **all of a sudden** plötzlich

T

(to) **take a look at** sich ansehen
talented [ˈtæləntɪd] talentiert
tan [tæn] (Sonnen-)Bräune
(to) **tap** [tæp] klopfen
thick [θɪk] dick
tobacco [təˈbækəʊ] Tabak
tone [təʊn] Ton
town square [ˈtaʊn skweə] Platz (in einer Stadt)
tray [treɪ] Tablett
truly [ˈtruːli]: **Yours truly** Hochachtungsvoll

(to) **turn** [tɜːn] werden; (to) **turn a corner** um die Ecke biegen; (to) **turn into** umwandeln in; (to) **turn out** herauskommen, resultieren
type [taɪp] Typ

U

(to) **understand** [ʌndəˈstænd] verstehen
unfortunately [ʌnˈfɔːtʃənətli] leider

V

verse [vɜːs] Strophe
violin [vaɪəˈlɪn] Violine

W

(to) **warm up** hochstarten, anlaufen
(to) **warn** [wɔːn] warnen
Well done Gut gemacht!
went: *s.p.* (to) **go "Ooh!"** „Ooh!" sagen; (to) **go along** mitgehen; (to) **go by** vorbeigehen; (to) **go wrong** schiefgehen
what: What's it all about? Um was geht es? **What's the matter?** Was ist los?
while [waɪl] Weile; **once in a while** manchmal
(to) **whisper** [ˈwɪspə] flüstern
who: Who am I to stand in your way? Warum sollte ich dir im Weg stehen?
why: Why, thank you Nun ja, danke
wide [waɪd] weit
wimp [wɪmp] Schwächling
within: within a week innerhalb einer Woche
worthless [ˈwɜːθləs] wertlos
writer [ˈraɪtə] Schriftsteller, Autor

Y

yeah [jeə] ja